# THE SCIENCE OF ATHLETIC PERFORMANCE

# THE SCIENCE OF ATHLETIC PERFORMANCE

FROM ANATOMY AND PHYSIOLOGY TO GENETICS, TRAINING, NUTRITION, PEDS, PSYCHOLOGY, RECOVERY AND INJURY PREVENTION, TECHNOLOGY, AND ENVIRONMENTAL FACTORS

ATHLETE DOMINATION

HADLEY MANNINGS

Copyright © 2022 by Hadley Mannings

All rights reserved. No part of this book may be reproduced, stored in a retrieval system, or transmitted in any form or by any means, electronic, mechanical, photocopying, recording, or otherwise, without the prior written permission of the publisher, Book Bound Studios.

The information contained in this book is based on the author's personal experiences and research. While every effort has been made to ensure the accuracy of the information presented, the author and publisher cannot be held responsible for any errors or omissions. The information in this book is not intended as medical or legal advice, and should not be used as such.

This book is intended for general informational purposes only and is not a substitute for professional medical or legal advice. If you have specific questions about any medical or legal matters, you should consult with a qualified healthcare professional or attorney.

Book Bound Studios is not affiliated with any product or vendor mentioned in this book. The views expressed in this book are those of the author and do not necessarily reflect the views of Book Bound Studios.

*To my family and friends, who have always supported me and believed in me. Thank you for your love and encouragement. This book would not have been possible without you.*

*Sincerely, Hadley Mannings*

"The body is a magnificent machine, capable of incredible feats of strength, endurance, and skill. It is up to us to hone and train this machine to its full potential, to push ourselves to be the best we can be."

UNKNOWN

# CONTENTS

| | |
|---|---|
| Foreword | xiii |
| Introduction | xv |
| 1. ANATOMY AND PHYSIOLOGY OF ATHLETIC PERFORMANCE | 1 |
| Unleashing the Power of Your Muscles | 1 |
| A Little Bit of Muscle Magic | 2 |
| Cardio and Breath: The Dynamic Duo of Athletic Performance | 4 |
| How Your Body Generates and Uses Energy During Exercise | 5 |
| Chapter Summary | 8 |
| 2. GENETICS AND ATHLETIC PERFORMANCE | 9 |
| Inherited Genetic Traits and Athletic Ability | 9 |
| Genetic Testing for Athletic Potential | 10 |
| Tailoring Training with Genetic Information | 11 |
| Ethical Considerations in the Use of Genetics in Sports | 13 |
| Chapter Summary | 15 |
| 3. TRAINING FOR ATHLETIC PERFORMANCE | 17 |
| The Principles of Training | 17 |
| The Benefits of Periodization and Variety in Training | 19 |
| The Role of Strength Training in Athletic Performance | 20 |
| Skill Development and Technique in Athletic Performance | 22 |
| Chapter Summary | 24 |
| 4. NUTRITION AND ATHLETIC PERFORMANCE | 25 |
| The Role of Nutrition in Athletic Performance | 25 |
| The Importance of Proper Hydration and Electrolyte Balance | 26 |

| | |
|---|---|
| The Role of Macronutrients in Athletic Performance | 27 |
| Micronutrients (Vitamins and Minerals) in Athletic Performance | 28 |
| Chapter Summary | 30 |

## 5. PERFORMANCE-ENHANCING SUBSTANCES AND DOPING — 31
Types of Performance-Enhancing Substances — 32
Risks and Consequences of Using Performance-Enhancing Substances — 33
Methods of Detecting and Preventing Doping in Sports — 34
Ethical Considerations in the Use of Performance-Enhancing Substances in Sports — 36
Chapter Summary — 39

## 6. PSYCHOLOGICAL FACTORS IN ATHLETIC PERFORMANCE — 41
The Role of Psychological Factors in Athletic Performance — 41
Stress and Anxiety in Athletic Performance and How to Manage Them — 42
Mental Skills Training in Athletic Performance — 43
Chapter Summary — 45

## 7. RECOVERY AND INJURY PREVENTION IN ATHLETIC PERFORMANCE — 47
Recovery and Injury Prevention in Athletic Performance — 47
The Different Types of Recovery Methods and Their Effectiveness — 48
Common Athletic Injuries and Strategies for Preventing Them — 50
Chapter Summary — 52

## 8. TECHNOLOGY AND ATHLETIC PERFORMANCE — 53
The Role of Technology in Athletic Performance — 53
Wearable Technology in Training and Competition — 54
Data Analysis and Performance Modeling in Athletic Performance — 55

| | |
|---|---|
| Potential Future Developments in Technology | 57 |
| Chapter Summary | 59 |
| 9. ENVIRONMENTAL FACTORS IN ATHLETIC PERFORMANCE | 61 |
| Altitude and Athletic Performance | 61 |
| Temperature and Athletic Performance | 62 |
| Humidity and Athletic Performance | 64 |
| Wind and Athletic Performance | 65 |
| Weather Conditions and Athletic Performance | 66 |
| Chapter Summary | 68 |
| Conclusion | 69 |
| Afterword | 71 |
| Acknowledgments | 73 |
| About the Author | 75 |

# FOREWORD

As the author of this book, I am honored to present it as a resource for improving your athletic performance. Whether you are a beginner or an experienced athlete, the information contained within these pages can help you achieve your goals and reach your full potential.

I have spent countless hours researching, writing, and revising this book. It will be a valuable resource as you strive to improve your athletic performance.

I want to take this opportunity to thank my family, friends, and colleagues who have supported and encouraged me throughout this process. Their guidance and encouragement have been invaluable, and I am forever grateful for their support.

This book will be a useful resource for you as you pursue your athletic goals, and I wish you all the best in your journey toward excellence.

Sincerely, Hadley Mannings

# INTRODUCTION

The science of athletic performance is a **complex** and **multifaceted** field that encompasses various disciplines, including anatomy and physiology, training, nutrition, psychology, and technology. Understanding the science behind the athletic performance is crucial for athletes who want to reach their full potential and achieve their goals.

This book will explore the key factors contributing to athletic performance and how we can optimize them. We will cover a wide range of topics, including the anatomy and physiology of athletic performance, genetics, training principles, nutrition, performance enhancing substances, psychological factors, recovery and injury prevention, the role of technology, and environmental factors.

## UNLEASHING YOUR INNER ATHLETE

A combination of physical, mental, and technical factors determines athletic performance. Physical factors include strength, power, endurance, and flexibility, which are influenced by genetics, training, and nutrition. Mental factors such as motivation, confidence, focus, and stress management can significantly impact athletic performance. Finally, technical factors such as technique and tactics can also play a crucial role in athletic performance, particularly in sports that require specific skills or strategies.

By understanding the science behind athletic performance, athletes and coaches can develop effective training programs, nutrition plans, and mental skills training tailored to the individual's specific needs and goals. This can help athletes optimize their physical and mental performance, reduce the risk of injury, and ultimately achieve their goals.

## SCOPE OF THE BOOK

This book is designed to provide a comprehensive overview of the key factors that contribute to athletic performance and how we can optimize them. We will delve into the anatomy and physiology of athletic performance, including the musculoskeletal system, the cardiovascular and respiratory systems, and the role of energy production and utilization. We will also explore training principles, including periodization, strength training, and skill development.

In addition to the physical aspects of athletic performance, we will also examine the psychological factors that can impact an athlete's performance, such as motivation, confidence, focus, and stress management. We will also discuss the importance of recovery and injury prevention in maintaining optimal performance. Finally, we will explore the role of technology in athletic performance, including wearable technology and data analysis to track and improve performance.

This introduction outlines the importance of understanding the science behind athletic performance and the book's scope. In the coming chapters, we will delve deeper into each of these topics, drawing upon the latest research and best practices to provide a comprehensive and practical guide to optimizing athletic performance. So, whether you are an athlete looking to improve your performance or a coach seeking to help your athletes reach their full potential, this book is designed to provide you with the knowledge and tools you need to succeed.

## CHAPTER 1
# ANATOMY AND PHYSIOLOGY OF ATHLETIC PERFORMANCE

The anatomy and physiology of athletic performance are crucial for **optimizing physical performance** and **minimizing the risk of injury**. In this chapter, we will explore the key systems and processes contributing to athletic performance, including the musculoskeletal system, muscle contractions, the cardiovascular and respiratory systems, and energy production and utilization.

## UNLEASHING THE POWER OF YOUR MUSCLES

The musculoskeletal system is a complex and intricate system essential for movement and force transfer. It comprises bones, joints, muscles, tendons, and ligaments, which work together to allow for movement and force production.

The bones provide a framework for the body and support the muscles, while the joints allow for movement between the bones. Several types of joints, including hinge joints, ball and socket joints, and pivot joints, allow for different types of movement. The bones are also important for storing minerals, such as calcium, and for producing blood cells.

The muscles are responsible for movement and the production of force. They produce force through contraction, and there are three muscle contractions: concentric, eccentric, and isometric. Concentric contractions involve the shortening of the muscle, eccentric contractions involve the lengthening of the muscle, and isometric contractions involve the static contraction of the muscle.

The tendons and ligaments connect the muscles to the bones and provide stability. The tendons attach the muscles to the bones and transfer force. At the same time, the ligaments connect the bones and provide stability to the joints.

The musculoskeletal system is central to athletic performance, as it is responsible for movement and force production. Strong, flexible, and well-coordinated muscles are essential for optimal athletic performance, and training programs should be designed to improve these qualities. Training programs should also focus on improving the strength and flexibility of the bones, joints, tendons, and ligaments to support the musculoskeletal system and prevent injuries.

By understanding the anatomy and function of the musculoskeletal system, athletes and coaches can develop training programs tailored to improve athletic performance and reduce the risk of injury.

## A LITTLE BIT OF MUSCLE MAGIC

Muscles produce force through contraction, and three muscle contractions can occur during exercise: concentric, eccentric, and isometric.

**Concentric contractions** occur when a muscle shortens as it contracts, such as when a bicep curls a dumbbell. During a concentric contraction, the muscle generates maximum force at its shortest length. This contraction is important for power and speed and is commonly used in jumping, throwing, and sprinting.

**Eccentric contractions** occur when a muscle lengthens as it contracts, such as when a bicep lowers a dumbbell back down. During an eccentric contraction, the muscle absorbs force at its longest length. This contraction can help improve muscle endurance and reduce the risk of injury, as it helps to decelerate and control movement.

**Isometric contractions** occur when a muscle maintains a constant length as it contracts, such as when a person holds a plank position. During an isometric contraction, the muscle generates force but does not change in length. This type of contraction is important for maintaining stability and balance, and it can also help to improve muscle strength and endurance.

Each type of muscle contraction has its unique benefits and can be trained to improve athletic performance. For example, concentric contractions are important for producing power and speed. In contrast, eccentric contractions can help improve muscle endurance and reduce the risk of injury. Finally, isometric contractions can help improve muscle strength, endurance, stability, and balance.

By understanding the different types of muscle contractions and their benefits, athletes and coaches can design training programs focusing on specific muscle contractions to improve athletic performance. For example, a sprinter may focus on training concentric contractions to improve speed. In contrast, an endurance athlete may focus on training eccentric contractions to improve muscle endurance.

It is also important to consider the balance between different types of muscle contractions in training programs. While each type of muscle contraction has its unique benefits, it is important to maintain a balance between concentric, eccentric, and isometric contractions to optimize athletic performance and prevent muscle imbalances.

Understanding how muscles produce force and the different muscle contractions during exercise is crucial for optimizing athletic performance. Athletes and coaches can design effective training programs that improve athletic performance by training specific muscle contractions and maintaining a balance between different contractions.

## CARDIO AND BREATH: THE DYNAMIC DUO OF ATHLETIC PERFORMANCE

The cardiovascular and respiratory systems play a crucial role in athletic performance. They deliver oxygen and nutrients to the muscles and remove waste products. The heart pumps oxygen-rich blood to the muscles through the circulatory system, while the lungs take in oxygen and release carbon dioxide through the respiratory system.

During exercise, the demand for oxygen and nutrients increases, and the cardiovascular and respiratory systems must work harder to deliver these essential nutrients to the muscles. As a result, the efficiency of these systems is a key factor in athletic performance, and training can improve their function and capacity.

We can train the cardiovascular system to improve efficiency through regular aerobic exercises like running, cycling, or swimming. This type of exercise helps to improve the function of the heart, lungs, and blood vessels, as well as increase the body's ability to deliver oxygen to the muscles. In addition, aerobic training can also improve the body's ability to remove waste products, such as lactic acid, from the muscles, which can help to reduce muscle fatigue.

We can also train the respiratory system to improve its efficiency through regular exercise and training techniques such as **deep breathing** and **diaphragmatic breathing**. These techniques can help improve the lungs' function and increase their capacity to take in oxygen.

In summary, the cardiovascular and respiratory systems play a crucial role in athletic performance, and training can improve their function and capacity. By training these systems through regular exercise and techniques such as deep breathing and diaphragmatic breathing, athletes and coaches can optimize athletic performance and improve the body's ability to deliver oxygen and nutrients to the muscles.

## HOW YOUR BODY GENERATES AND USES ENERGY DURING EXERCISE

Energy production and utilization are other important aspects of athletic performance. The body uses a combination of carbohydrates, fats, and proteins as fuel during exercise, and the type and intensity of the activity will determine which energy systems are primarily used.

The phosphagen system is the primary energy system for high-intensity, short-duration activities, such as sprinting or weightlifting. This system uses stored ATP (adenosine triphosphate) and creatine phosphate to produce energy rapidly. Still, it can only sustain high-intensity exercise for a short period. **ATP is the primary source of energy for the body**, and it is stored in the muscles and other tissues. Creatine phosphate is also stored in the muscles and regenerates ATP during exercise.

The glycolytic system is used for moderate-intensity, moderate-duration activities like running or cycling. This system breaks down glycogen (a carbohydrate stored in the muscles) to produce energy. It can sustain moderate-intensity exercise for longer periods. However, it also produces lactic acid as a byproduct, which can lead to **muscle fatigue**. Glycogen is stored in the muscles and liver, and we can break it down into glucose, which the body uses to produce energy.

The oxidative system is used for low-intensity, long-duration activities like distance running or cycling. This system uses fat and carbohydrate stores to produce energy and sustain low-intensity exercise for extended periods. However, it is less efficient than the other energy systems and produces energy at a slower rate. The oxidative system relies on the breakdown of fats and carbohydrates to produce energy. Therefore, it is primarily used during low-intensity, long-duration exercise.

**Optimizing energy production and utilization is crucial for athletic performance**, and training and nutrition can play a significant role in this process. By understanding how the body produces and uses energy during exercise, athletes and coaches can develop effective training programs and nutrition plans tailored to the individual's specific needs.

For example, an athlete training for a marathon may focus on increasing their glycogen stores and improving their body's ability to use fat as fuel during long-duration exercise. On the other hand, a sprinter may focus on increasing their ATP stores and improving their body's ability to produce energy quickly and efficiently through the phosphagen system.

Understanding how the body produces and uses energy during exercise is crucial for optimizing athletic performance. By training the different energy systems and optimizing nutrition, athletes and coaches can improve the body's ability to produce and utilize energy efficiently. This can help to improve performance, reduce fatigue, and enhance recovery.

It is also important to consider the balance between different energy systems in training programs. While each energy system has unique benefits, it is important to maintain a balance between the phosphagen, glycolytic, and oxidative systems to optimize athletic performance and prevent muscle imbalances.

In this chapter, we have explored the anatomy and physiology of athletic performance and how they contribute to optimal physical performance. By understanding the musculoskeletal system, muscle contractions, the cardiovascular and respiratory systems, and energy production and utilization, athletes and coaches can develop effective training programs and nutrition plans tailored to the individual's specific needs and goals.

## CHAPTER SUMMARY

- The musculoskeletal system is essential for movement and force production and includes bones, joints, muscles, tendons, and ligaments.
- The bones provide a framework for the body and support the muscles, while the joints allow for movement between the bones.
- The muscles produce force through contraction, and there are three muscle contractions: concentric, eccentric, and isometric.
- Concentric contractions involve the shortening of the muscle, eccentric contractions involve the lengthening of the muscle, and isometric contractions involve the static contraction of the muscle.
- Tendons and ligaments connect the muscles to the bones and provide stability.
- Training programs should focus on improving the strength, flexibility, and coordination of the muscles and the strength and flexibility of the bones, joints, tendons, and ligaments.
- The cardiovascular and respiratory systems deliver oxygen and nutrients to the muscles during exercise.
- Energy production and utilization are important for athletic performance, as the body requires energy to perform physical activity. The body primarily uses carbohydrates and fats as fuel sources, and the balance between the two depends on the intensity and duration of the activity.

## CHAPTER 2
# GENETICS AND ATHLETIC PERFORMANCE

The study of genetics involves examining how traits are inherited from one generation to the next. In the context of athletic performance, genetics plays a role in determining an individual's physical characteristics and abilities, such as **muscle structure**, **metabolism**, and **cardiovascular function**. While genetics is only one factor that contributes to athletic performance, it can significantly impact an athlete's potential and the sports in which they are best suited.

## INHERITED GENETIC TRAITS AND ATHLETIC ABILITY

Inherited genetic traits can impact an individual's athletic ability in various ways. Some genetic traits linked to athletic performance include muscle fiber type, VO2 max, and muscle strength.

**Muscle fiber** type is a genetic trait that determines the type of muscle fibers an individual has in their body. Fast-twitch muscle fibers are responsible for short bursts of explosive power. In contrast, slow-twitch fibers are better suited for endurance activities. Individuals with a higher proportion of fast-twitch fibers may be more suited to power-based sports, such as sprinting or weightlifting. In comparison, those with a higher proportion of slow-twitch fibers may excel in endurance sports like marathon running or cycling.

**VO2 max** measures the body's ability to use oxygen and is often associated with endurance performance. Individuals with a high VO2 max can take in and use more oxygen during exercise, allowing them to sustain higher activity levels for longer periods. Genetics can play a role in an individual's VO2 max, with some people having a higher VO2 max than others.

**Muscle strength** is another genetic trait that can impact athletic performance. Strength is determined by the size and number of muscle fibers, as well as the efficiency of the nervous system in activating those fibers. Therefore, individuals with a strong genetic predisposition for muscle strength may have an advantage in sports that require strength and power, such as football or rugby.

It is important to note that while genetics can play a role in determining an individual's athletic ability, other factors, such as training, nutrition, and environment, also play a significant role in athletic performance. Therefore, by understanding the impact of inherited genetic traits on athletic ability, coaches and athletes can better tailor training programs and make informed decisions about which sports and events to pursue.

## GENETIC TESTING FOR ATHLETIC POTENTIAL

Genetic testing has become increasingly popular in recent years to predict athletic potential and tailor training programs. However, it is important to understand that **genetic testing is just one tool in the toolkit and should not be relied upon as the sole determinant of an athlete's potential.**

Genetic testing involves analyzing an individual's DNA to identify variations in specific genes that are thought to be related to athletic performance. Some common genes tested include ACTN3, which is associated with muscle fiber type, and PPARA, which is involved in fat metabolism.

While genetic testing can provide some insight into an individual's athletic potential, it is important to recognize the limitations of this type of testing. The relationship between genetics and athletic performance is complex and multifaceted, and genetic testing can only provide a partial picture. Training, nutrition, and environmental conditions also play a significant role in athletic performance. Therefore, we cannot capture them through genetic testing alone.

Additionally, the accuracy of genetic testing can vary, and the results may only sometimes be reliable. Therefore, it is important for athletes and coaches to work with qualified professionals and to interpret genetic test results in the context of other factors that may impact athletic performance.

In summary, genetic testing can provide useful information for predicting athletic potential and tailoring training programs. Still, it should not be relied upon as the sole determinant of an athlete's potential. Therefore, it is important to consider the limitations of genetic testing and to interpret the results in the context of other factors that impact athletic performance.

## TAILORING TRAINING WITH GENETIC INFORMATION

Using genetic information to tailor training programs is a relatively new area of research in athletic performance. While genetic testing can provide some insight into an individual's athletic potential and how they may respond to different types of training, it is important to recognize this approach's limitations and consider other factors that may impact training response.

One potential use of genetic information in training is identifying an individual's muscle fiber type and tailoring training accordingly. For example, individuals with a higher proportion of fast-twitch muscle fibers may benefit from more explosive, power-based training. In comparison, those with a higher proportion of slow-twitch fibers may respond better to endurance-based training. However, it is important to note that muscle fiber type is just one factor that can impact training response. Other factors, such as training history, nutrition, and overall training load, play a role.

Another potential use of genetic information in training is identifying an **individual's risk for overtraining or injury**. For example, some genetic variations have been linked to an increased risk of overtraining or certain types of injuries. By identifying these risk factors, coaches and athletes can adjust training programs and implement strategies to prevent overtraining and injuries. However, it is important to recognize that genetics is just one factor among many that can impact the risk of overtraining or injury and that other factors, such as training load, technique, and recovery strategies, also play a role.

In summary, using genetic information to tailor training programs is a promising area of research. Still, it is important to recognize this approach's limitations and consider other factors that may impact training response. It is also important to work with qualified professionals and to interpret genetic test results in the context of an individual's overall training program.

## ETHICAL CONSIDERATIONS IN THE USE OF GENETICS IN SPORTS

The use of genetics in sports raises several ethical considerations, including discrimination, privacy, and fairness issues.

One concern is the potential for genetic discrimination in sports. If genetic testing becomes widespread, there is a risk that athletes with certain genetic traits may be unfairly excluded from certain sports or events. For example, an athlete with a genetic predisposition for muscle strength may be unfairly excluded from a weight class in a sport such as wrestling or weightlifting, even if they meet all other requirements for competition.

Another concern is the potential for the misuse of genetic information in sports. There is a risk that coaches or trainers may use genetic information to advantage certain athletes unfairly or to exclude others unfairly. This could create an uneven playing field and undermine the integrity of the competition.

There are also concerns about privacy and the potential for misusing genetic information outside sports. For example, suppose athletes undergo genetic testing as part of their training. In that case, they may risk having their genetic information accessed or used without their consent.

To address these concerns, sports organizations need to establish clear guidelines and policies for using genetic testing in sports. This could include measures to protect athletes' privacy and ensure that genetic information is not used to advantage or disadvantage athletes unfairly. It may also be necessary to establish an oversight body to monitor genetic testing in sports and ensure that it is used ethically and responsibly.

In summary, the use of genetics in sports raises several ethical considerations that must be carefully considered and addressed to ensure that the rights and interests of athletes are protected.

In conclusion, genetics plays a role in athletic performance by determining an individual's physical characteristics and abilities. Certain inherited genetic traits, such as muscle fiber type, VO2 max, and muscle strength, can impact an athlete's athletic ability and the sports in which they are best suited. As a result, genetic testing has become popular for predicting athletic potential and tailoring training programs. Still, it is important to recognize this approach's limitations and consider other factors that may impact athletic performance. In addition, genetics in sports raises several ethical considerations, including discrimination, privacy, and fairness issues. Therefore, sports organizations need to establish clear guidelines and policies for using genetic testing in sports to ensure that the rights and interests of athletes are protected. Overall, understanding genetics's role in athletic performance can help coaches and athletes make informed decisions about training and competition.

## CHAPTER SUMMARY

- Genetics plays a role in determining an individual's physical characteristics and abilities that impact athletic performance.
- Inherited genetic traits that can impact athletic ability include muscle fiber type, VO2 max, and muscle strength.
- Fast-twitch muscle fibers are responsible for short bursts of explosive power. In contrast, slow-twitch fibers are better suited for endurance activities.
- VO2 max measures the body's ability to use oxygen and is often associated with endurance performance.
- Strength is determined by the size and number of muscle fibers, as well as the efficiency of the nervous system in activating those fibers.
- Genetic testing involves analyzing an individual's DNA to identify variations in specific genes that are thought to be related to athletic performance.
- Genetic testing can provide useful information for predicting athletic potential and tailoring training programs. Still, it is just one tool and should not be relied upon as the sole determinant of an athlete's potential.
- Other factors, such as training, nutrition, and environment, also play a significant role in athletic performance.

## CHAPTER 3
# TRAINING FOR ATHLETIC PERFORMANCE

Training is a crucial aspect of athletic performance, and understanding the principles of training and how they apply to athletic performance is essential for optimizing physical and technical performance. In this chapter, we will explore the key training principles and how we can use them to improve athletic performance.

## THE PRINCIPLES OF TRAINING

Training involves systematically applying stress to the body to stimulate adaptation and improve physical and technical performance. Several key training principles apply to athletic performance, including overload, specificity, progression, and reversibility.

**Overload** is applying greater stress or demand on the body than it is accustomed to stimulating adaptation. For example, lifting progressively heavier weights or progressively running longer distances can overload the muscles and stimulate adaptation. The body will adapt to the increased demand by becoming stronger, faster, or more endurance-oriented. Applying the appropriate overload level is important, as too much can lead to overtraining and injury, while too little may not provide a sufficient stimulus for adaptation.

**Specificity** refers to the principle of training specifically for the demands of the sport or activity. Sports or activities have different physical and technical demands, and training should be specific to these demands to optimize performance. For example, a sprinter must train muscles to produce maximal force quickly. In contrast, distance runners must train their muscles to produce low-intensity, long-duration force.

**Progression** refers to gradually increasing the intensity or volume of training in a controlled and systematic manner. Progression allows the body to adapt to the increasing demands of training and avoid overtraining or injury. Therefore, it is important to progressively increase the intensity or volume of training in a controlled and logical manner rather than increasing it too quickly.

**Reversibility** refers to the principle that if training is stopped or significantly reduced, the adaptations gained from training will begin to decline. Therefore, maintaining a consistent training program is essential for maintaining the adaptations gained from training. For example, suppose athletes take a significant break from training. In that case, they may lose some of the strength, endurance, or other physical qualities they gained through training. This is why it is important to maintain a consistent training program to maintain the adaptations gained from training.

In summary, the principles of training are important for optimizing athletic performance. By understanding and applying the principles of overload, specificity, progression, and reversibility, athletes and coaches can develop effective training programs tailored to the individual athlete's specific needs and goals. These principles help ensure that training is effective, efficient, and safe and can help athletes reach their full potential and succeed in their sport.

## THE BENEFITS OF PERIODIZATION AND VARIETY IN TRAINING

Periodization is the systematic planning and organization of training over some time. It involves dividing the training year into blocks or phases, each with a specific focus or goal. Periodization allows athletes to vary their training and avoid overtraining or boredom. In addition, it can help athletes peak for important competitions or events.

Several types of training can be used as part of a periodized training program, including endurance, strength, power, speed, skill development, and recovery.

**Endurance training** involves training the body's ability to sustain prolonged physical activity. It is important for sports that involve long-distance or sustained effort, such as running, cycling, or swimming. Endurance training can improve the efficiency of the cardiovascular and respiratory systems, as well as the muscles' ability to use oxygen and produce energy.

**Strength training** involves using resistance exercises to improve muscle size, strength, and power. In addition, strength training can improve athletic performance by increasing the force production capabilities of the muscles and improving bone density and joint stability.

**Power training** involves exercises that produce maximum force in the shortest time, such as plyometrics or Olympic lifts. Power training can improve explosive power and speed, which can be important for sports that require quick bursts of force, such as basketball, soccer, or football.

**Speed training** involves exercises focusing on improving

movement speed, such as sprinting or agility drills. Speed training can improve athletic performance by increasing movement speed and the body's ability to change direction quickly.

**Skill development** involves practicing and refining specific technical skills, such as throwing, hitting, or shooting. Skill development is crucial for sports that require specific technical skills, and we can improve it through deliberate practice and repetition.

**Recovery** is an important aspect of training, as it allows the body to repair and adapt to training demands. Recovery can include rest, massage, or active recovery exercises, which are important for maintaining optimal performance and reducing the risk of injury.

In conclusion, periodization is a crucial aspect of training that helps athletes and coaches organize and structure training to optimize performance and avoid overtraining. By dividing the training year into blocks or phases with specific goals and focuses, athletes can vary their training and peak for important competitions or events. Several types of training can be used as part of a periodized training program, including endurance, strength, power, speed, skill development, and recovery. By understanding the different types of training and how we can use them in a periodized program, athletes and coaches can develop effective training programs tailored to the individual athlete's specific needs and goals.

## THE ROLE OF STRENGTH TRAINING IN ATHLETIC PERFORMANCE

Strength training is a type of training that involves the use of resistance exercises to improve muscle size, strength, and power. Strength training can be an important aspect of athletic performance, as it can improve the muscles' force production capabilities and bone density, and joint stability.

Several strength training exercises can improve athletic performance, including free weights, machines, and bodyweight exercises. Free weights, such as dumbbells, barbells, and kettlebells, allow for a greater range of movement and can be more effective for improving functional strength. Machines, such as weight machines or cable machines, provide a more controlled movement and can be useful for targeting specific muscle groups. Finally, bodyweight exercises, such as push-ups, squats, and lunges, use the body's weight as resistance and can improve functional strength.

**The intensity, volume, and frequency of strength training should be carefully planned and progressively increased to allow for optimal adaptation and avoid overtraining or injury.** Strength training should be specific to the needs and goals of the individual, and it should be integrated into a well-rounded training program that includes other types of training, such as endurance, power, and skill development.

In conclusion, strength training is an important aspect of athletic performance that can improve the muscles' force production capabilities, bone density, and joint stability. Several strength training exercises can improve athletic performance, including free weights, machines, and bodyweight exercises. The intensity, volume, and frequency of strength training should be carefully planned and progressively increased to allow for optimal adaptation and avoid overtraining or injury. Strength training should be specific to the needs and goals of the individual, and it should be integrated into a well-rounded training program that includes other types of training, such as endurance, power, and skill development. By understanding the role of strength training in athletic performance and how to incorporate it into a training program effectively, athletes and coaches can optimize athletic performance and reach their full potential.

## SKILL DEVELOPMENT AND TECHNIQUE IN ATHLETIC PERFORMANCE

Athletic performance heavily depends on the technical skills required by the sport or activity. Whether it's throwing a ball with precision, hitting it with power, or shooting it with accuracy, the ability to execute these skills with proper technique is essential for success. This is why skill development and technique are so important in athletic performance.

**Deliberate practice** is a key component of skill development. This involves focusing on specific skills or techniques and practicing them to improve. **Repetition** is also important, as it allows the body to ingrain the proper movement patterns and muscle memory needed for proper technique. Coaches and trainers can help athletes develop skills through various methods, including verbal cues, demonstrations, and feedback.

The technique is another important aspect of athletic performance. Proper technique can help improve the efficiency and effectiveness of a skill, as well as reduce the risk of injury. Coaches and trainers can help athletes refine their technique through verbal cues, demonstrations, and feedback. We can also use technology to track and improve techniques, such as video analysis or wearable sensors.

In conclusion, skill development and technique are essential for optimal athletic performance. Deliberate practice and repetition are key components of skill development. Proper technique can improve efficiency and reduce the risk of injury. Coaches and trainers are crucial in helping athletes develop and refine their skills and technique. Technology can also be a useful tool in this process.

This chapter has explored the key training principles and how they apply to athletic performance. We have discussed the importance of periodization in training and the different types of training that can be used to optimize performance, including endurance, strength, power, speed, skill development, and recovery. We have also examined the role of strength training in athletic performance and the importance of skill development and technique in optimizing technical performance. By understanding the principles of training and how they apply to athletic performance, athletes and coaches can develop effective training programs tailored to the individual's specific needs and goals. In the coming chapters, we will delve deeper into the role of nutrition in athletic performance and how it can be optimized to support training and performance.

## CHAPTER SUMMARY

- Training involves applying stress to the body to stimulate adaptation and improve physical and technical performance.
- Key training principles include overload, specificity, progression, and reversibility.
- Overload involves applying greater stress or demand on the body than it is accustomed to.
- Specificity involves training specifically for the demands of the sport or activity.
- Progression involves gradually increasing the intensity or volume of training in a controlled and systematic manner.
- Reversibility refers to the principle that if training is stopped or significantly reduced, the adaptations gained from training will begin to decline.
- Periodization is the systematic planning and organization of training over time. It involves dividing the training year into blocks or phases with specific focuses or goals.
- Several types of training can be used in a periodized training program, including endurance, strength, power, speed, skill development, and recovery.

## CHAPTER 4
# NUTRITION AND ATHLETIC PERFORMANCE

Proper nutrition is essential for optimal athletic performance, as it supports the body's ability to recover from training, repair and build new tissues, and produce energy. In this chapter, we will explore the role of nutrition in athletic performance and how it can be optimized to support training and performance.

## THE ROLE OF NUTRITION IN ATHLETIC PERFORMANCE

Nutrition is a complex and multifaceted aspect of athletic performance. Athletes need to understand the specific nutritional needs of their sport and their bodies to optimize their performance. This includes understanding the role of different macronutrients, such as carbohydrates, proteins, and fats, as well as the importance of micronutrients, such as vitamins and minerals.

**Carbohydrates** are the body's primary energy source during exercise and should be most athletes' primary fuel source. Carbohydrates can be found in various foods, such as grains, fruits, and vegetables. We should consume them appropriately based on the intensity and duration of the activity.

**Protein** is important for building and repairing tissues. Therefore, it is especially important for athletes who engage in high-intensity or strength-based training. Good protein sources include meat, poultry, fish, beans, and dairy products.

**Fats** are also an important energy source for the body and are necessary for maintaining healthy skin, hair, and joints. Fats can be found in foods such as nuts, seeds, and avocados, and we should consume them in appropriate amounts.

**Micronutrients**, such as vitamins and minerals, are essential for maintaining good health and optimal athletic performance. They can be found in various foods, such as fruits, vegetables, and fortified foods. Therefore, we should consume them appropriately to meet the body's needs.

Proper nutrition is essential for athletic performance. Therefore, athletes should work with a registered dietitian or sports nutritionist to develop a nutrition plan that meets their specific needs and goals.

## THE IMPORTANCE OF PROPER HYDRATION AND ELECTROLYTE BALANCE

Proper hydration is essential for athletic performance. It supports the body's ability to regulate temperature, transport nutrients and oxygen, and remove waste products. Dehydration can significantly impact athletic performance, leading to fatigue, muscle cramps, and impaired mental function.

Athletes should **aim to drink enough fluids to replace any fluids lost through sweat during exercise** and drink before, during, and after exercise to maintain hydration. Water is the primary fluid needed for hydration. Still, athletes may also need to replace electrolytes, such as sodium and potassium, lost through sweat. Sports drinks and electrolyte supplements can replace electrolytes during prolonged or intense exercise.

## THE ROLE OF MACRONUTRIENTS IN ATHLETIC PERFORMANCE

Macronutrients are nutrients that the body needs in large amounts and include carbohydrates, proteins, and fats. Each macronutrient plays a unique role in athletic performance and can be important for optimizing energy production, repair and recovery, and body composition.

**Carbohydrates** are the body's primary energy source and are important for athletic performance, particularly high-intensity or endurance activities. Carbohydrates can be stored in the muscles and liver as glycogen, which we can break down to produce energy during exercise. Therefore, consuming adequate amounts of carbohydrates before, during, and after exercise can help maintain glycogen stores and support energy production.

**Proteins** are important for building and repairing tissues, such as muscles. They are also involved in the production of enzymes and hormones. Therefore, adequate protein intake is important for athletic performance, as it can support muscle repair, growth, and immune function.

**Fats** are an important source of energy and are also important for hormone production and cell membrane structure. Fats can be used as an energy source during exercise, particularly during low-intensity or endurance activities. However, excess intake of fats can lead to weight gain and negatively impact athletic performance.

The specific macronutrient needs of athletes depend on the demands of the sport, the intensity and duration of the training, and the individual's goals. Therefore, athletes should work with a sports dietitian or nutritionist to determine their specific macronutrient needs and how they can be met through a balanced diet and supplements, if necessary.

## MICRONUTRIENTS (VITAMINS AND MINERALS) IN ATHLETIC PERFORMANCE

Micronutrients are nutrients that the body needs in small amounts, including vitamins and minerals. These nutrients play important roles in various physiological processes and can be important for athletic performance.

**Vitamins** are essential for the proper functioning the body's systems and can be important for athletic performance. For example, vitamin C is important for immune function, and vitamin D is important for bone health. Vitamin E is an antioxidant that can help protect cells from oxidative stress caused by intense exercise. Vitamin K is important for blood clotting and bone health.

**Minerals** are essential for various physiological processes, such as electrolyte balance and muscle contraction. Therefore, mineral deficiencies can negatively impact athletic performance. Therefore, if necessary, athletes must consume adequate minerals through a balanced diet or supplements. Some important minerals for athletic performance include calcium, which is important for bone health, and sodium and potassium, which help regulate electrolyte balance and muscle contractions. Iron is also important for oxygen transport to the muscles, and a deficiency can lead to fatigue and impaired performance.

Athletes must consume a varied and balanced diet that includes adequate micronutrients and macronutrients such as carbohydrates, proteins, and fats. Individual needs may vary based on the type and intensity of the sport, as well as the athlete's age, gender, and training status. Working with a sports dietitian can help athletes determine their specific nutrient needs and develop a personalized nutrition plan.

In summary, micronutrients are important for various physiological processes that support athletic performance. Therefore, adequate intake of micronutrients through a varied and balanced diet or supplements can help optimize performance and reduce the risk of deficiencies or health problems. If necessary, athletes must pay attention to their micronutrient intake and work with a sports dietitian to ensure optimal nutrition.

In this chapter, we have explored the role of nutrition in athletic performance and how it can be optimized to support training and performance. We have discussed the importance of proper hydration, electrolyte balance, and macronutrients, such as carbohydrates, proteins, and fats, in athletic performance. We have also examined the role of micronutrients, such as vitamins and minerals, in athletic performance. By understanding the role of nutrition in athletic performance, athletes and coaches can develop effective nutrition plans tailored to the individual's specific needs and goals.

## CHAPTER SUMMARY

- Proper nutrition is essential for optimal athletic performance. It supports the body's ability to recover from training, repair and build new tissues, and produce energy.
- Macronutrients, such as carbohydrates, proteins, and fats, are nutrients that the body needs in large amounts and play unique roles in athletic performance.
- Carbohydrates are the body's primary energy source and are important for high-intensity or endurance activities.
- Proteins are important for building and repairing tissues and are involved in the production of enzymes and hormones.
- Fats are an important source of energy and are also important for hormone production and cell membrane structure.
- Micronutrients, such as vitamins and minerals, are essential for maintaining good health and optimal athletic performance.
- Proper hydration is essential for athletic performance. It supports the body's ability to regulate temperature, transport nutrients and oxygen, and remove waste products.
- Athletes should aim to drink enough fluids to replace any fluids lost through sweat during exercise and drink before, during, and after exercise to maintain hydration. They may also need to replace electrolytes lost through sweat.

# CHAPTER 5
# PERFORMANCE-ENHANCING SUBSTANCES AND DOPING

Performance-enhancing substances, also known as **performance-enhancing drugs** (PEDs), are substances that are taken to improve athletic performance. These include legal and illegal substances, such as anabolic steroids, stimulants, and hormone supplements. PEDs, also known as doping, is a controversial topic in sports. They can give athletes an unfair advantage and undermine the integrity of the competition. While some athletes may use PEDs to gain a competitive edge, using these substances can have serious risks and consequences, including increased risk of injury, long-term health problems, and even death in some cases. As a result, PEDs are strictly prohibited in many sports and are subject to strict penalties and sanctions. To protect the health and well-being of athletes and maintain the integrity of competition, sports organizations have implemented various methods for detecting and preventing doping, including testing programs and education initiatives.

## TYPES OF PERFORMANCE-ENHANCING SUBSTANCES

Performance-enhancing substances, or performance-enhancing drugs (PEDs), are substances that are taken to improve athletic performance. Many different types of PEDs can have a range of effects on athletic performance. Some common types of PEDs include:

**Anabolic steroids:** Anabolic steroids are synthetic hormones that mimic the effects of testosterone in the body. Athletes often use these substances to increase muscle mass, strength, and endurance. However, anabolic steroids can have serious side effects, including liver damage, heart problems, and hormonal imbalances.

**Stimulants:** Stimulants are substances that increase energy levels and alertness. Common stimulants used as PEDs include caffeine, amphetamines, and ephedrine. These substances can have various side effects, including increased heart rate, hypertension, and insomnia.

**Hormone supplements:** Hormone supplements, such as human growth hormone (HGH) and erythropoietin (EPO), increase muscle mass and endurance. HGH is a hormone that is naturally produced by the body. At the same time, EPO is a hormone that stimulates the production of red blood cells. Hormone supplements can have serious side effects, including an increased risk of cancer, heart problems, and kidney damage.

**Diuretics:** Diuretics are substances that increase urine production, which can help reduce weight and increase muscle definition. However, diuretics can also cause dehydration, electrolyte imbalances, and other health problems.

**Masking agents:** Masking agents are substances used to prevent the detection of other PEDs in drug testing. These substances can include substances that interfere with drug testing procedures or that are used for flushing PEDs out of the body. Masking agents are strictly prohibited in many sports and can result in significant penalties and sanctions.

In summary, many different types of performance-enhancing substances can have a range of effects on athletic performance. Therefore, athletes need to be aware of the risks and consequences of using PEDs and the strict penalties and sanctions we can impose for doping. In addition to the physical risks associated with PED use, athletes caught using these substances may face significant legal and professional consequences, including disqualification from the competition, loss of sponsorships, and damage to their reputation. Therefore, it is important for athletes to understand the risks and consequences of using PEDs and to make informed decisions about whether to use these substances.

## RISKS AND CONSEQUENCES OF USING PERFORMANCE-ENHANCING SUBSTANCES

Performance-enhancing substances, or performance-enhancing drugs (PEDs), can have a range of risks and consequences for athletes. Some of the potential risks and consequences of using PEDs include the following:

**Physical risks:** PEDs can have a range of physical risks and side effects, depending on the specific substance and the method of use. Some common risks associated with PED use include liver damage, heart problems, hormonal imbalances, and an increased risk of injury. In some cases, the use of PEDs can even be fatal.

**Legal consequences:** PEDs are strictly prohibited in many sports and are subject to strict penalties and sanctions. Athletes caught using PEDs may face disqualification from the competition, loss of titles and awards, and fines. In some cases, using PEDs may also be illegal and can result in criminal charges.

**Professional consequences:** PEDs can have significant professional consequences for athletes, including loss of sponsorships, damage to their reputation, and difficulty finding future sports opportunities. In addition to the financial implications of these consequences, the loss of professional opportunities can be emotionally and mentally challenging for athletes.

**Ethical implications:** Using PEDs raises several ethical concerns, including issues related to fairness and the integrity of the competition. Athletes who use PEDs may be seen as cheating and undermining the trust of their peers, fans, and the wider community.

**Psychological consequences:** PEDs can have psychological consequences for athletes, including increased pressure to perform, guilt, and shame. Athletes caught using PEDs may also face social ostracism and struggle to rebuild their reputation and credibility.

In summary, using PEDs can have serious risks and consequences for athletes, including physical, legal, professional, ethical, and psychological implications. Therefore, it is important for athletes to be aware of these risks and consequences and to make informed decisions about whether to use PEDs.

## METHODS OF DETECTING AND PREVENTING DOPING IN SPORTS

To maintain the integrity of competition and protect the health and well-being of athletes, sports organizations have implemented various methods for detecting and preventing doping in sports. Some common methods for detecting and preventing doping include:

**Drug testing:** Drug testing is a commonly used method for detecting the use of performance-enhancing substances in sports. Drug testing can be conducted through urine, blood, or other types of samples and detect the presence of a wide range of PEDs. Independent agencies typically conduct drug testing. It follows strict protocols to ensure the accuracy and reliability of the results.

**Education and awareness programs:** Many sports organizations and governing bodies have implemented education and awareness programs to educate athletes about the risks and consequences of doping and to promote fair play. These programs can include information about the types of PEDs prohibited, the risks and consequences of using these substances, and the methods used to detect and prevent doping.

**Therapeutic Use Exemptions (TUEs):** In some cases, athletes may have a legitimate medical need for a substance that is otherwise prohibited in their sport. In these cases, athletes can apply for a Therapeutic Use Exemption (TUE) to use the substance for therapeutic purposes. TUEs are granted a case-by-case basis and require strict documentation and oversight to prevent abuse.

**In-competition and out-of-competition testing:** Many sports organizations conduct both in-competition and out-of-competition testing to detect the use of PEDs. In-competition testing occurs during actual competition and is designed to detect the use of PEDs that may have a performance-enhancing effect during the event. Out-of-competition testing occurs outside competition and is designed to detect the use of PEDs that may have a long-term performance-enhancing effect or to identify doping patterns. Out-of-competition testing allows sports organizations to test athletes more frequently and can deter doping more effectively.

**Biological Passport:** The Biological Passport is a program that uses long-term monitoring of an athlete's biological markers to detect the use of PEDs. The Biological Passport involves collecting and analyzing multiple athletes' samples over time to create a profile of their normal levels of certain markers. If the levels of these markers deviate from the athlete's normal profile, it may indicate PED use. The Biological Passport is used in conjunction with traditional drug testing. It is considered to be a more effective deterrent to doping.

In summary, various methods are used to detect and prevent doping in sports, including drug testing, education and awareness programs, Therapeutic Use Exemptions (TUEs), in-competition and out-of-competition testing, and the Biological Passport. These methods are designed to protect athletes' health and well-being and maintain the integrity of competition in sports.

## ETHICAL CONSIDERATIONS IN THE USE OF PERFORMANCE-ENHANCING SUBSTANCES IN SPORTS

The use of performance-enhancing substances, or performance-enhancing drugs (PEDs), in sports raises several ethical considerations. Some of the ethical issues related to the use of PEDs in sports include the following:

**Fairness:** PEDs can give athletes an unfair advantage over their competitors, undermining the fairness of competition. This can be particularly problematic in individual sports, where one athlete's performance can directly affect the event's outcome. Using PEDs can also create uncertainty in competition, as it is difficult to know whether an athlete's performance is the result of natural ability or the use of PEDs.

**Health risks:** Using PEDs can have serious health risks for athletes, including long-term health problems and even death in some cases. Using PEDs can also create an unhealthy culture in sports, where athletes feel pressured to take risks with their health to succeed.

**Professional integrity:** Using PEDs can damage athletes' professional integrity and undermine the trust of fans, sponsors, and the wider community. Athletes caught using PEDs may face significant consequences, including loss of titles, awards, and sponsorships and damage to their reputation.

**Legal implications:** The use of PEDs can have legal implications for athletes, as the possession, use, and distribution of certain PEDs may be illegal in some jurisdictions. Athletes caught using PEDs may face criminal charges in addition to the sanctions imposed by their sport.

**Personal autonomy:** Using PEDs raises questions about personal autonomy and the right of athletes to make their own decisions about their bodies and careers. Some may argue that athletes should have the freedom to decide whether to use PEDs. In contrast, others may argue that the risks and consequences of PED use are too great and that athletes should be protected from making potentially harmful decisions. This complex ethical issue requires balancing the rights of athletes to make their own decisions with the need to protect the health and well-being of athletes and the integrity of the competition.

In conclusion, using performance-enhancing substances in sports raises several ethical considerations, including fairness, health risks, professional integrity, legal implications, and personal autonomy. Therefore, it is important for athletes, coaches, and sports organizations to consider these ethical issues when making decisions about using PEDs and to strive for fair and ethical practices in sports.

This chapter explored the performance-enhancing substances used in sports, including anabolic steroids, stimulants, hormone supplements, diuretics, and masking agents. We also examined the risks and consequences of using these substances, including the physical risks, legal and professional consequences, and ethical considerations. Finally, we discussed the methods used to detect and prevent doping in sports, including drug testing, education and awareness programs, Therapeutic Use Exemptions (TUEs), in-competition and out-of-competition testing, and the Biological Passport.

It is important for athletes, coaches, and sports organizations to be aware of the risks and consequences of using PEDs and to strive for fair and ethical practices in sports. By understanding the impact of PEDs on athletic performance and the methods used to detect and prevent doping, we can work towards a more fair and ethical sports culture.

## CHAPTER SUMMARY

- Performance-enhancing substances, also known as performance-enhancing drugs (PEDs), are substances taken to improve athletic performance.
- PEDs include legal and illegal substances, such as anabolic steroids, stimulants, hormone supplements, diuretics, and masking agents.
- PEDs can give athletes an unfair advantage and undermine the integrity of competition.
- PEDs can have serious risks and consequences, including increased risk of injury, long-term health problems, and even death in some cases.
- PEDs are strictly prohibited in many sports and are subject to strict penalties and sanctions.
- Sports organizations have implemented methods for detecting and preventing doping, including testing programs and education initiatives.
- Risks and consequences of using PEDs include physical risks, legal and professional consequences, and ethical considerations.
- To ensure fair competition and protect the health and well-being of athletes, it is important for athletes to understand the risks and consequences of using PEDs and to make informed decisions about whether to use these substances.

## CHAPTER 6
# PSYCHOLOGICAL FACTORS IN ATHLETIC PERFORMANCE

Psychological factors can significantly impact athletic performance, and understanding their role and how to optimize them can be crucial for optimal performance. This chapter will explore the psychological factors affecting athletic performance and how we can manage them to improve performance.

## THE ROLE OF PSYCHOLOGICAL FACTORS IN ATHLETIC PERFORMANCE

Psychological factors, such as **motivation**, **confidence**, **focus**, **stress**, and **anxiety**, can significantly impact athletic performance. These factors can affect an athlete's ability to perform to their full potential. Both internal and external factors can influence them.

**Motivation** is an important psychological factor affecting athletic performance, as it drives an athlete's desire and determination to succeed. Motivation can be influenced by various factors, including personal goals, feedback from coaches and teammates, and the desire to succeed.

**Confidence** is another important psychological factor that can impact athletic performance. Confidence is an athlete's belief in their ability to succeed. It can be influenced by past performance, support from others, and training and preparation.

**Focus** is the ability to concentrate and direct attention, which is important for athletic performance, particularly in sports requiring mental focus and decision-making. Conversely, distractions or lack of focus can negatively impact performance, and techniques such as visualization or pre-performance routines can help athletes maintain focus.

**Stress** and **anxiety** can also affect athletic performance, as they can interfere with an athlete's ability to perform to their full potential. Stress and anxiety can be caused by various internal and external factors, such as pressure to perform, fear of failure, or physical or mental fatigue.

## STRESS AND ANXIETY IN ATHLETIC PERFORMANCE AND HOW TO MANAGE THEM

The role of stress and anxiety in athletic performance is complex, as both can have positive and negative effects on an athlete's performance. On the one hand, a certain stress level can act as a motivator, helping athletes focus and perform at their best. However, on the other hand, if stress and anxiety reach unmanageable levels, they can become detrimental to performance.

Stress and anxiety can impact athletic performance by interfering with an athlete's ability to concentrate, focus, and make decisions. This can be particularly problematic in sports that require split-second decisions or quick reactions. Chronic stress and anxiety can also lead to physical and mental fatigue, negatively impacting performance.

There are several strategies that athletes can use to manage stress and anxiety and improve performance. One effective technique is **relaxation training**, which can include *deep breathing, progressive muscle relaxation,* or *meditation*. These techniques help athletes relax and focus their attention, which can benefit performance. In addition, mental skills training, such as goal setting or visualization, can help manage stress and anxiety.

Suppose an athlete is struggling with stress and anxiety. In that case, they need support from a coach, sports psychologist, or mental health professional. These individuals can help athletes develop healthy coping strategies and manage stress and anxiety. It is also important for athletes to maintain a healthy lifestyle, including getting enough sleep, eating a balanced diet, and engaging in regular physical activity. This can help athletes manage their stress and anxiety levels and improve their overall performance.

## MENTAL SKILLS TRAINING IN ATHLETIC PERFORMANCE

Mental skills training can be particularly useful for athletes competing in high-pressure situations, such as championship games or close contests. In these situations, mental skills training can help athletes maintain their focus and concentration and prevent distractions from affecting their performance.

Mental skills training can also be helpful for athletes who are recovering from injury or facing setbacks in their careers. By developing mental skills such as goal setting and positive self-talk, athletes can stay motivated and focused on their long-term goals, even during difficult times.

**Athletes need to be proactive in their mental skills training, as it can take time to develop and refine these skills.** Athletes should be committed to practicing and refining their mental skills regularly. They should be open to seeking guidance and support from coaches, sports psychologists, or other mental skills professionals. Athletes can improve their overall performance and achieve their full potential in their sport by investing in their mental skills training.

In this chapter, we have explored the psychological factors affecting athletic performance and how we can manage them to optimize performance. We have discussed the importance of motivation, confidence, and focus in athletic performance, the role of stress and anxiety, and how to manage them. We have also examined the importance of mental skills training in athletic performance and how we can incorporate it into an athlete's training program. By understanding the psychological factors that can impact athletic performance and how to optimize them, athletes and coaches can develop strategies to improve mental performance and manage stress and anxiety. In the next chapter, we will explore the role of genetics in athletic performance and how it can impact an athlete's potential and development.

## CHAPTER SUMMARY

- Psychological factors, such as motivation, confidence, focus, stress, and anxiety, can significantly impact athletic performance.
- Stress and anxiety can interfere with an athlete's ability to concentrate, focus, and make decisions.
- Relaxation techniques, such as deep breathing, progressive muscle relaxation, and meditation, can help athletes manage stress and anxiety and improve performance.
- Mental skills training, including goal setting and visualization, can help athletes manage stress and anxiety and improve performance.
- Athletes need to seek support from a coach, sports psychologist, or mental health professional if they struggle with stress and anxiety.
- Maintaining a healthy lifestyle, including getting enough sleep, eating a balanced diet, and engaging in regular physical activity, can help athletes manage stress and anxiety and improve overall performance.
- Team cohesion, or unity and cooperation within a team, can also impact athletic performance.
- Techniques such as communication skills training and team bonding activities can help improve team cohesion and enhance performance.

CHAPTER 7
# RECOVERY AND INJURY PREVENTION IN ATHLETIC PERFORMANCE

Recovery and injury prevention are crucial for optimal athletic performance, as they support the body's ability to adapt and improve from training. They also reduce the risk of injury. This chapter will explore the importance of recovery and injury prevention in athletic performance and discuss strategies for optimizing recovery and preventing injuries.

## RECOVERY AND INJURY PREVENTION IN ATHLETIC PERFORMANCE

Recovery and injury prevention are essential aspects of athletic performance, as they allow the body to repair and adapt to the demands of training and competition. Proper recovery and injury prevention strategies can help athletes maintain optimal performance, reduce the risk of injury, and prevent overtraining.

Athletes can use several recovery methods to support their bodies and optimize performance, including **active recovery**, **passive recovery**, **nutrition**, and **sleep**. Active recovery involves low-intensity activities such as light stretching or yoga, which can help the body recover and improve flexibility. Passive recovery methods, such as massage or ice baths, can help reduce inflammation and muscle soreness. Adequate nutrition and hydration are also important for recovery, as they provide the body with the necessary nutrients and fluids to repair and rebuild tissues. Finally, sleep is crucial for recovery, as it allows the body to repair and regenerate tissues and replenish energy stores.

Injury prevention is also important in athletic performance, as **injuries can significantly impact an athlete's ability to train and compete**. There are several strategies that athletes can use to prevent injuries, including warm-up and cool-down routines, proper technique, and the use of protective equipment. Proper technique is particularly important, as poor technique can increase the risk of injury. Athletes should also be aware of their bodies, listen to any warning signs of potential injuries, such as pain or discomfort, and seek medical attention if necessary.

In summary, recovery and injury prevention is essential for optimal athletic performance. By understanding the different types of recovery methods and strategies for injury prevention, athletes and coaches can develop effective training programs that support the body and reduce the risk of injury.

## THE DIFFERENT TYPES OF RECOVERY METHODS AND THEIR EFFECTIVENESS

Recovery and injury prevention are crucial for optimal athletic performance, as they allow the body to repair and rebuild tissues that have been damaged during training, as well as reduce the risk of injury. In addition, proper recovery and injury prevention strategies can help athletes maintain a consistent training program, which is essential for maintaining the adaptations gained from training.

Athletes can use several recovery methods to optimize recovery and prevent injuries, including active recovery, passive recovery, nutrition, and sleep. Active recovery involves low-intensity exercise or movement that helps to flush out waste products and improve circulation, such as walking or light stretching. Passive recovery involves rest, such as massage or cold water immersion. It can be effective in reducing muscle soreness and inflammation.

**Proper nutrition** is also crucial for recovery, providing the body with the necessary nutrients for repairing and rebuilding tissues. Adequate intake of carbohydrates, proteins, and fluids can help support recovery and reduce muscle soreness. Adequate sleep is also important for recovery, allowing the body to repair and rebuild tissues and support immune function. Lack of sleep can negatively impact athletic performance and increase the risk of injury.

**Injury prevention** is also an important aspect of athletic performance, and there are several strategies that athletes can use to reduce the risk of injury. These strategies include proper warm-up and cool-down techniques, using proper technique and form during training, and using appropriate equipment and protective gear. In addition, strength training and flexibility training can also help to improve muscle balance and reduce the risk of injury.

It is important for athletes to find a balance between recovery and training and to incorporate a variety of recovery methods into their training program. By prioritizing recovery and injury prevention, athletes can optimize their performance and reduce the risk of setbacks.

## COMMON ATHLETIC INJURIES AND STRATEGIES FOR PREVENTING THEM

Athletic injuries are common and can significantly impact athletic performance. Common athletic injuries include muscle strains, sprains, and stress fractures.

We can use several strategies to prevent athletic injuries, including proper training and conditioning, warm-up and cool-down, and proper technique and form. Wearing appropriate protective equipment, such as helmets or mouthguards, can also help reduce the risk of injury.

Proper training and conditioning can help reduce the risk of injury by building strength and flexibility and gradually increasing the intensity and duration of training. Proper warm-up and cool-down routines can also help reduce the risk of injury by preparing the body for exercise and helping to reduce muscle soreness and fatigue.

Proper technique and form are important for preventing injuries, particularly in sports that involve specific technical skills. Coaches and trainers can play a crucial role in teaching proper technique and form and providing feedback to athletes to help them improve their technique.

In addition to these strategies, **athletes must listen to their bodies** and recognize when they are feeling tired or experiencing pain. Overuse injuries, such as tendonitis or stress fractures, can often be prevented by taking breaks and allowing the body to rest and recover. Regular stretching and foam rolling can also help reduce the risk of injury by improving flexibility and mobility.

Proper nutrition and hydration are also important for injury prevention. They can support the body's immune system and help maintain optimal physical function. In addition, adequate intake of nutrients, such as protein, carbohydrates, and electrolytes, can help support muscle repair and recovery. In contrast, proper hydration can help maintain optimal muscle function and prevent cramping.

Finally, athletes need to **seek medical attention** if they experience an injury. Early diagnosis and treatment can help prevent the injury from worsening and speed up recovery. Physical therapists and athletic trainers can also be valuable resources for helping athletes recover from injuries and preventing future injuries.

In this chapter, we have explored the importance of recovery and injury prevention in athletic performance and discussed strategies for optimizing recovery and preventing injuries. We have examined the different recovery methods and their effectiveness and discussed common athletic injuries and prevention strategies. By understanding the importance of recovery and injury prevention and how to optimize them, athletes and coaches can develop effective strategies to maintain physical and mental well-being and optimize performance.

## CHAPTER SUMMARY

- Recovery and injury prevention is essential for optimal athletic performance, as they allow the body to repair and adapt to the demands of training and competition.
- Recovery methods include active recovery (low-intensity exercise or movement), passive recovery (rest), nutrition, and sleep.
- Proper nutrition is important for recovery, providing the body with the necessary nutrients for repairing and rebuilding tissues.
- Adequate sleep is also crucial for recovery, allowing the body to repair and rebuild tissues and support immune function.
- Strategies for injury prevention include proper warm-up and cool-down techniques, proper technique and form during training, and appropriate equipment and protective gear.
- Strength and flexibility training can also help prevent injuries by improving muscle strength and balance.
- Working with a coach or sports medicine professional can help athletes develop an effective recovery and injury prevention plan.
- Athletes need to listen to their bodies and seek medical attention to prevent injuries from worsening.

## CHAPTER 8
# TECHNOLOGY AND ATHLETIC PERFORMANCE

Technology has significantly impacted athletic performance and how athletes train and compete. In this chapter, we will explore the role of technology in athletic performance and discuss the use of wearable technology, data analysis, and performance modeling, as well as the potential future developments in technology and their impact on athletic performance.

## THE ROLE OF TECHNOLOGY IN ATHLETIC PERFORMANCE

Technology has played an increasingly significant role in athletic performance in recent years. From wearable sensors to video analysis software, technology can provide athletes with valuable insights and data that can help them optimize their training and performance.

One of the primary ways that technology has impacted athletic performance is through **wearable sensors**, such as fitness trackers or GPS watches. These devices can give athletes real-time data on their physical activity, including heart rate, distance traveled, and burned calories. We can use this information to monitor training intensity, track progress, and adjust training programs.

**Video analysis software** is another technology that has significantly impacted athletic performance. This software allows athletes and coaches to review and analyze video footage of training sessions or competitions to identify strengths, weaknesses, and areas for improvement. Video analysis can be particularly useful for sports that involve specific technical skills, such as throwing, hitting, or shooting, as it can provide insights into an athlete's technique and form.

Technology has also impacted how coaches and trainers communicate and interact with athletes. For example, apps and software can provide a platform for coaches to share training programs, schedules, and other important information with athletes and facilitate communication and feedback.

Overall, technology has had a significant impact on athletic performance, and it is likely to continue to play a major role in the future. By leveraging the power of technology, athletes and coaches can gain valuable insights and data that can help optimize training and performance.

## WEARABLE TECHNOLOGY IN TRAINING AND COMPETITION

Wearable technology, such as fitness trackers, smartwatches, and GPS devices, have become increasingly popular in recent years and have been adopted by many athletes for training and competition purposes. Wearable technology can provide athletes with valuable data and insights that can help improve their performance and track their progress.

One common use of wearable technology in training is to track and monitor physical activity. Wearable devices can track various metrics, such as heart rate, steps taken, distance traveled, and calories burned, which can help athletes monitor their training intensity and volume. Wearable devices can also provide feedback on technique, such as stride length and cadence, which can help athletes optimize their training and improve their performance.

In competition, athletes can use **wearable technology to monitor performance and track progress in real-time**. For example, GPS devices can provide athletes with speed, distance, and pacing data, which can help them optimize their performance and make strategic decisions during a race. Wearable devices can also give athletes real-time feedback on their technique, such as swing speed or stroke rate, which can help them make adjustments and improve their performance.

Wearable technology can also be used to **monitor recovery and prevent injuries**. For example, wearable devices can track sleep quality and heart rate variability, providing valuable insights into an athlete's recovery status. Wearable devices can also alert if an athlete is at risk of overtraining or needing a break to recover.

Overall, wearable technology has the potential to significantly improve athletic performance by providing athletes with valuable data and insights that can help them optimize their training, track their progress, and monitor their recovery. However, it is important for athletes to carefully consider the types of wearable technology most suitable for their needs and use them responsibly and thoughtfully.

## DATA ANALYSIS AND PERFORMANCE MODELING IN ATHLETIC PERFORMANCE

The use of data analysis and performance modeling has become increasingly prevalent in the world of athletics as coaches and athletes seek to gain a competitive edge through the use of data-driven approaches. Data analysis involves collecting and interpreting data to inform decision-making and performance. We can use it in various ways to improve athletic performance.

One way data analysis can be used in athletics is by **tracking physical performance data**, such as speed, power, and endurance. Wearable technology, such as GPS tracking devices and heart rate monitors, can collect this data and provide insights into an athlete's physical capabilities and training needs. By analyzing this data, coaches and athletes can identify areas of strength and weakness and develop targeted training programs to improve performance.

**Performance modeling** is another way data analysis can be used in athletics. Performance modeling involves using mathematical models and algorithms to predict an athlete's future performance based on past performance data. This can be useful for predicting the outcomes of competitions and developing training programs tailored to an athlete's specific needs and goals.

Data analysis and performance modeling can also **inform tactical decision-making in team sports**. By analyzing data on an opponent's strengths and weaknesses, coaches can develop strategies that exploit their own team's strengths and exploit their opponent's weaknesses. Data analysis can also be used to inform the player selection and substitution decisions, as well as to identify areas of the game where the team needs to improve.

Overall, athletic data analysis and performance modeling can provide valuable insights and help coaches and athletes make informed decisions about training and competition. As a result, athletes and coaches can optimize performance and gain a competitive edge by leveraging data and technology.

## POTENTIAL FUTURE DEVELOPMENTS IN TECHNOLOGY

There are several potential future developments in technology that could impact athletic performance in the coming years. One of these developments is using **artificial intelligence (AI) and machine learning in sports analytics and performance modeling**. AI and machine learning algorithms can analyze large amounts of data, such as athlete performance data, to identify patterns and trends that we can use to optimize training and performance.

Another potential future technological development is **virtual reality** (VR) and **augmented reality** (AR) in training and competition. We can use VR and AR to simulate real-world environments and scenarios, allowing athletes to train in a more realistic and immersive environment. VR and AR can also be used to improve coaching and analysis, as they can provide a more accurate and detailed view of an athlete's performance.

Wearable technology is also expected to continue to evolve and improve, potentially developing more advanced sensors and devices that can track and analyze a wider range of physiological and performance data. These devices could provide athletes with real-time feedback and guidance, helping them optimize their performance.

Another potential future technological development is using **biometric sensors and smart clothing**. Biometric sensors can track and analyze various physiological parameters, such as heart rate and body temperature, and smart clothing can incorporate these sensors into garments that we can wear during training and competition. This technology could provide athletes with more accurate and detailed data about their body's responses to exercise, allowing them to optimize their training and performance.

Overall, future technological developments are expected to

significantly impact athletic performance in the coming years, providing athletes with new tools and technologies to optimize their training and performance. Therefore, it is important for athletes and coaches to stay up-to-date with these developments and to consider how we can use them to enhance performance.

In this chapter, we have explored the role of technology in athletic performance and discussed the use of wearable technology, data analysis, and performance modeling. We have also examined the potential future technological developments and their impact on athletic performance. By understanding the role of technology in athletic performance and the potential future developments, athletes and coaches can develop strategies to optimize performance and training.

## CHAPTER SUMMARY

- Technology has had a significant impact on athletic performance, including the use of wearable sensors, data analysis software, and performance modeling.
- Wearable technology, such as fitness trackers and GPS watches, can provide athletes with data on their physical activity, including heart rate and distance traveled, to optimize training intensity and track progress.
- Video analysis software allows athletes and coaches to review and analyze video footage of training sessions and competitions to identify areas for improvement.
- Apps and software can provide a platform for coaches to communicate with athletes and share training programs and schedules.
- Athletes can also use wearable technology in competition to monitor performance and track progress in real-time.
- Wearable devices can track sleep quality and heart rate variability to monitor recovery and prevent injuries.
- Data analysis and performance modeling can help athletes and coaches identify trends and predict future performance.
- Future developments in technology, such as virtual reality and biometric sensors, have the potential to impact athletic performance further.

## CHAPTER 9
# ENVIRONMENTAL FACTORS IN ATHLETIC PERFORMANCE

Several factors influence athletic performance, including genetics, training, nutrition, and psychology. In addition to these internal factors, external environmental conditions can significantly impact athletic performance. Environmental conditions such as altitude, temperature, humidity, and wind can affect an athlete's physical abilities. They can have a direct impact on the outcome of a sporting event. This chapter will explore how environmental conditions impact athletic performance and how athletes can prepare for and adapt to these conditions.

## ALTITUDE AND ATHLETIC PERFORMANCE

Altitude is a key environmental factor that can impact athletic performance. Altitude refers to the height above sea level at which an athlete is training or competing. At higher altitudes, the air is thinner and contains less oxygen, which can affect an athlete's physical abilities.

The impact of altitude on athletic performance is due to the physiological changes in the body when exposed to a lower oxygen environment. The body must work harder to obtain oxygen at higher altitudes, leading to increased heart rate, ventilation, and blood flow. These physiological changes can affect an athlete's physical abilities, including endurance, strength, and power.

The effects of altitude on athletic performance can vary depending on the individual athlete and the specific sport. Some athletes may be more affected by altitude than others, and certain sports may be more impacted by altitude than others. For example, endurance sports, such as running, cycling, and triathlon, may be more affected by altitudes than power sports, such as football or basketball.

There are several strategies that athletes can use to prepare for and adapt to the effects of altitude. One approach is to **train at a high altitude for some time before competing at altitude**. This can help the body adapt to the lower oxygen environment and improve athletic performance. Other strategies include using **oxygen supplements** or **sleeping in hypoxic tents**, which simulate high altitude conditions.

Altitude is a key environmental factor that can impact athletic performance. The physiological changes in the body at high altitudes can affect an athlete's physical abilities, and the impact of altitude can vary depending on the athlete and the specific sport. Therefore, athletes can optimize their performance at altitude by understanding the effects of altitude and using strategies to prepare for and adapt to high altitude conditions.

## TEMPERATURE AND ATHLETIC PERFORMANCE

Temperature is another environmental factor that can impact athletic performance. The body's internal temperature must be regulated to maintain optimal physical and mental function. When the body becomes too hot or cold, it can affect an athlete's physical abilities and performance.

Generally, the **optimal temperature for athletic performance** is around **68-72 degrees Fahrenheit (20-22 degrees Celsius)**. However, the body may overheat at temperatures above this range, leading to increased heart rate, sweating, and fatigue. This can affect an athlete's endurance, strength, and power and may increase the risk of heat-related illness.

On the other hand, the body may begin to cool down at temperatures below this range, leading to decreased heart rate, blood flow, and muscle function. This can affect an athlete's physical abilities and increase the risk of injury. Cold temperatures can also affect an athlete's mental function and focus, making it more difficult to perform at their best.

There are several strategies that athletes can use to prepare for and adapt to different temperature conditions. For example, athletes can stay hydrated in hot temperatures, wear lightweight and breathable clothing, and seek shade or use cooling devices to help regulate their body temperature. In cold temperatures, athletes can wear layers of clothing, use hand and foot warmers, and perform dynamic stretches to help keep their muscles warm and flexible.

In summary, the temperature is an important environmental factor that can impact athletic performance. By understanding the effects of temperature on the body and using strategies to prepare for and adapt to different temperature conditions, athletes can optimize their performance and reduce the risk of heat-related illness or injury.

## HUMIDITY AND ATHLETIC PERFORMANCE

Humidity, or the amount of moisture in the air, is another environmental factor that can impact athletic performance. High humidity levels can affect an athlete's physical abilities and performance by making it more difficult for the body to regulate its internal temperature.

When the air is humid, sweat does not evaporate from the skin as easily, making it harder for the body to cool down. This can lead to increased heart rate, sweating, and fatigue, affecting an athlete's endurance, strength, and power. High humidity levels can also make breathing more difficult, affecting an athlete's cardiovascular function and performance.

On the other hand, low humidity levels can lead to dehydration and decreased sweating, affecting an athlete's ability to regulate their body temperature and increasing the risk of heat-related illness.

There are several strategies that athletes can use to prepare for and adapt to different humidity levels. For example, athletes can stay hydrated in high-humidity conditions, wear lightweight and breathable clothing, and use cooling devices to help regulate their body temperature. In low-humidity conditions, athletes can drink electrolyte-rich fluids and use moisturizing products to prevent dry skin.

In summary, humidity is an important environmental factor impacting athletic performance. By understanding the effects of humidity on the body and using strategies to prepare for and adapt to different humidity levels, athletes can optimize their performance and reduce the risk of heat-related illness or dehydration.

## WIND AND ATHLETIC PERFORMANCE

The wind is another environmental factor that can impact athletic performance. Wind can affect an athlete's physical abilities and performance in several ways, depending on the strength and direction of the wind and the specific sport being played.

For example, in sports that involve throwing or hitting a ball, such as a baseball, golf, or tennis, wind can affect the trajectory and distance of the ball. In addition, wind can affect an athlete's speed and energy expenditure in running and cycling, with headwinds making it more difficult to move forward and tailwinds providing a boost. In outdoor sports, wind can also affect an athlete's balance and stability, making it more difficult to maintain control.

There are several strategies that athletes can use to prepare for and adapt to wind conditions. For example, in sports that involve throwing or hitting a ball, athletes can practice in windy conditions to develop the skills and techniques needed to compensate for wind. In running and cycling, athletes can adjust their pace and strategy based on the wind direction and strength. Finally, athletes can use crouching or a lower center of gravity in outdoor sports to maintain balance and stability in windy conditions.

In summary, the wind is an environmental factor that can impact athletic performance in various sports. By understanding the effects of wind on physical abilities and performance and using strategies to prepare for and adapt to wind conditions, athletes can optimize their performance and maintain control in windy conditions.

## WEATHER CONDITIONS AND ATHLETIC PERFORMANCE

Weather conditions, such as temperature, humidity, and wind, can all impact athletic performance. In addition to these factors, other types of weather, such as **rain**, **snow**, and **lightning**, can also affect athletic performance.

Rain can affect an athlete's grip and traction, as well as their visibility and concentration. In sports involving running, jumping, or throwing, rain can make the field or surface slippery, increasing the risk of injury and affecting an athlete's physical abilities. In sports that involve handling a ball or equipment, rain can make the ball or equipment wet and slippery, affecting an athlete's grip and control.

Snow can affect an athlete's traction and stability, as well as their visibility and concentration. In sports involving running, jumping, or throwing, snow can make the field or surface slippery, increasing the risk of injury and affecting an athlete's physical abilities. In sports that involve handling a ball or equipment, snow can make the ball or equipment cold and hard, affecting an athlete's grip and control.

Lightning poses a significant safety risk to athletes, especially in outdoor sports. When lightning is present, athletes must seek shelter and avoid playing or practicing until the storm has passed.

There are several strategies that athletes can use to prepare for and adapt to different weather conditions. For example, athletes can wear appropriate footwear and clothing in rainy or snowy conditions to improve traction and stability. In sports that involve handling a ball or equipment, athletes can use strategies such as using a different grip or adjusting the way they throw or hit the ball to compensate for wet or slippery conditions. In the event of lightning, athletes should follow established protocols for seeking shelter and avoiding play or practice until the storm has passed.

In summary, weather conditions, including temperature, humidity, wind, rain, snow, and lightning, can all impact athletic performance. By understanding the effects of different weather conditions on physical abilities and performance and using strategies to prepare for and adapt to different weather conditions, athletes can optimize their performance and reduce the risk of injury.

This chapter has explored how environmental factors, such as altitude, temperature, humidity, wind, and weather conditions, can impact athletic performance. These factors can affect an athlete's physical abilities and performance, depending on the sport played and the specific environmental conditions.

Altitude, for example, can affect an athlete's oxygen uptake and cardiovascular function. At the same time, temperature and humidity can impact their ability to regulate their body temperature and stay hydrated. In addition, wind can affect an athlete's speed and trajectory. In contrast, weather conditions like rain, snow, and lightning can affect an athlete's traction, stability, and visibility.

By understanding the impact of environmental factors on athletic performance and using strategies to prepare for and adapt to different conditions, athletes can optimize their performance and reduce the risk of injury. Athletes, coaches, and sports organizations need to be aware of how environmental factors can impact athletic performance and take steps to mitigate their impact.

## CHAPTER SUMMARY

- Environmental conditions such as altitude, temperature, humidity, and wind can impact athletic performance.
- Altitude affects athletic performance due to physiological changes in the body caused by thinner air with less oxygen at higher altitudes. These changes can affect endurance, strength, and power.
- Athletes can prepare for and adapt to high altitude conditions by training at high altitudes beforehand or using oxygen supplements or hypoxic tents.
- The optimal temperature for athletic performance is around 68-72 degrees Fahrenheit (20-22 degrees Celsius). Higher temperatures can lead to increased heart rate, sweating, and fatigue. In comparison, lower temperatures can lead to decreased heart rate, blood flow, and muscle function.
- Humidity can impact athletic performance by affecting the body's ability to regulate its temperature through sweating. High humidity makes sweat harder to evaporate and cool the body, leading to increased heat stress and fatigue.
- Wind can affect athletic performance by increasing the effort required to move through it, particularly in sports such as running and cycling. Wind can also affect the trajectory and movement of objects in sports such as golf, baseball, and tennis.
- To prepare for and adapt to different environmental conditions, athletes can use strategies such as staying hydrated, wearing appropriate clothing, using cooling or warming devices, and performing dynamic stretches.

# CONCLUSION

This book explores the science behind athletic performance and the various factors that can impact athletic performance. We have examined the anatomy and physiology of athletic performance and how the musculoskeletal, cardiovascular, and respiratory systems contribute to athletic performance. We have also discussed training principles and the importance of periodization, strength training, and skill development in athletic performance.

We have explored the role of nutrition in athletic performance, the importance of proper hydration and electrolyte balance, and the role of macronutrients and micronutrients in athletic performance. We have also examined the psychological factors that can impact athletic performance, such as motivation, confidence, focus, stress, and anxiety, and how we can manage them to optimize performance.

We have discussed the importance of recovery and injury prevention in athletic performance and the various methods and strategies we can use to optimize recovery and prevent injuries. We have also examined the role of technology in athletic performance and the use of wearable technology, data analysis, and performance modeling.

In conclusion, understanding the science behind athletic performance is crucial for optimizing training and performance. By understanding the various factors impacting athletic performance and how we can manage them, athletes and coaches can develop strategies to optimize training and performance.

# AFTERWORD

I am grateful for the opportunity to share my knowledge and insights on athletic performance. The information presented in this book has been useful and informative for readers. In addition, it has helped shed light on the factors that impact athletic performance and how to optimize them.

I express my sincere gratitude to everyone who has supported and encouraged me throughout writing this book. My family, friends, and colleagues, thank you for your love and support. To my readers, thank you for your interest in this topic and for taking the time to read my work.

I hope this book has inspired readers to continue learning and growing as athletes and trainers and to always strive for excellence in their pursuit of athletic performance. Thank you for joining me on this journey, and I hope to see you again in future endeavors.

Sincerely, Hadley Mannings

# ACKNOWLEDGMENTS

I want to express my gratitude to all those who have contributed to the creation and publication of this work.

First and foremost, I would like to thank my mentors and advisors, who have provided guidance and support throughout the research and writing process. Their expertise and encouragement have been invaluable to me.

I also want to thank my colleagues and peers who have offered support, feedback, and encouragement throughout this journey. Their insights and perspectives have helped shape and improve my work.

I want to thank my family and friends for their love and support during the long hours of research and writing. Their encouragement and understanding have kept me motivated and on track.

Finally, I would like to thank the publishing team for their work in bringing this book to fruition. Their professionalism and attention to detail have been instrumental in completing this project.

Thank you all for your contribution to this work.

Sincerely, Hadley Mannings

## ABOUT THE AUTHOR

Hadley Mannings is an avid athlete and coach with over 10 years of experience in the field. He has a passion for helping athletes reach their full potential and has dedicated his career to studying the science behind athletic performance. In his book, he shares his knowledge and insights on the various factors that impact athletic performance, including anatomy and physiology, training principles, nutrition, and mental skills training. In his free time, he enjoys competing in triathlons and coaching young athletes in track and field.

www.ingramcontent.com/pod-product-compliance
Lightning Source LLC
Chambersburg PA
CBHW072103110526
44590CB00018B/3300